The Way of the Birds

A child and a curlew
travel across the world

Written by Meme McDonald

Illustrated by Shane Nagle

A
LITTLE
ARK
BOOK

ALLEN & UNWIN

for Grace and Brenna
who travelled the way of the birds
before they could walk

        M.M.

for Arianna

   S.N.

Come close. Listen.

This story is about a girl and a curlew.
Watch and wait. Travel across the
world with them to places on the
edge of memory.

Breathe in. Breathe out.

In a breathless moment before the dawn you were born. Your eyes were wide. So wide. Watching. Breathe in, breathe out. Listening for distant sounds beyond the rush of morning traffic. Waiting.

Beneath soft blankets one tiny finger moved, toes wriggled and then the whole of your newborn body stretched. A perfectly formed mouth opened wide. Your cry was like the call of a bird travelling high overhead. Your mother smiled and stroked your cheek. Contented, you drifted back to sleep.

Your baby days were long and slow. Eating and sleeping, waking, eating and sleeping. Dirtying nappies, crying and smiling. A cheeky, round face with freckles appeared over the edge of your cot.

You kicked your feet wildly, flapping your arms. Your big brother pretended to goo and gurgle, then brummmed and niaouwed and ratatattatted, bombarding your cot with soft toys, making the bells and bright colours jangle. Sometimes you were frightened and cried. Then your mother would come rushing and the cheeky, round face would run away.

Birds flew past your window. You called to them. Loud calls. Not screams, but screeches. Like the screeches of a cockatoo. Your mother laughed with friends and neighbours.

'She's copying the old cocky down the road.'

They laughed and tickled you under the chin.

'Chubby thing. One day you'll grow feathers and fly away!'

One year passed. You clambered to your feet and toddled outside to roll on the grass by the bay, and sing to the birds overhead.

Another year passed. Still you called out like a cockatoo. Still you rolled on the grass and sang to the birds. You walked and ran, jumped and threw balls, played games and drew pictures. But never spoke a word.

Then your mother stopped laughing at your bird calls. For hours she tried to teach you to speak in words. As the years passed, she sometimes shouted at you to speak like an ordinary human being.

She grew worried and sad. Neighbours tried to help, shaping the words slowly as they pointed to cats and dogs. Doctors looked down your throat and in your ears. They asked you to draw pictures of yourself, your favourite foods, and to build houses out of blocks. They could find nothing that made you like a bird. Everything was just as it should be for a young girl. Except your voice.

You felt sorry for your mother. You stayed quiet.

Now people treat you like you are dumb. Except your brother. He looks after you and talks to you till late at night from the top bunk. He says not to worry, lots of what people say doesn't make sense anyway. He reads you stories and often shares his secrets. He likes to talk a lot. When he gets sent to his room for being rude or for not doing jobs round the house, you sing to him, sweet songs of the birds. His tears stop and he hums along, drifting into sleep.

In the mornings you climb onto the top bunk while your brother is still sleeping. You bounce up and down, screeching. He moans and then tickles and you run for your life.

You watch him getting ready for school. You fiddle with his coloured pencils, twirling them between your fingers, watching the colours spin. You dream of sitting in class with other children. Your brother gets impatient and yells.

And then he is gone and you face the day alone. Other children your age hurry past the front fence with their school bags. You hide. You wander out the back, picking up twigs until you find just the right one to draw squiggles in the dirt – bird tracks. Whenever birds pass overhead you dance and whirl and call to the wind. You dream of places far beyond your own backyard.

As the sun gets heavy in the sky, you find some paper and the pencil you hid that morning. You sit on the front steps, drawing, waiting for the distant sound of the school bell that will bring your brother home.

He jostles you as he comes through the gate. On special days he brings you presents – treasures he finds in the dirt, or feathers. You play and fight and then it's time to leave him alone, your mother says.

'He's got to do his homework!'

If he finishes in time before dinner, you drag him out the back, jump on the handlebars of his bike, and whinge until he pedals you round the corner and down the street to the verandah where old man cockatoo sits in his cage. You speak with the wise, old bird. Sometimes you cry. That's when your brother says it's time to go home, dinner is ready and he's starving. If one of his mates rides by, your brother nudges you sharply to be quiet. He doesn't like it much when friends stare. It's then that you long for the wings to fly away.

One day, everything changes.
It's lunchtime. You are chasing sultanas
round the plate with a crust of toasted cheese
that growls like a tiger. Suddenly, you feel a rush of
wind on your face. The wind becomes stronger,
making you dizzy. Your mother tells you to sit down.

'Come on, eat up your lunch!'

But the sandwich becomes a blur and your
mother's voice blown and tossed about. You call
out. A long, mournful call. Then you rush about the
house losing balance and crashing into things. You
can feel yourself falling, dropping from the sky.

Your brother is still at school.

Your mother's strong arms try to hold you
still, stroking, calming, but you fling yourself
free and rush out the back to the furthest
corner. There you clamber in among the
broken bricks and unwanted bits of timber
and tin. You fall heavily onto a patch of earth
and cry as if your heart is broken.

Still shaking, you look up. Not far away
something moves, beating the earth in a
panic, then resting, struggling some more,
then giving up. Through a blur of tears you
see a stretched wing, then the whole bird. A
very big bird, fallen to the ground here in
the rubble. Its feathers are brown and buff.
It has a delicate, curved beak, a slender
neck and long legs. Your mother sighs
and wanders back inside.

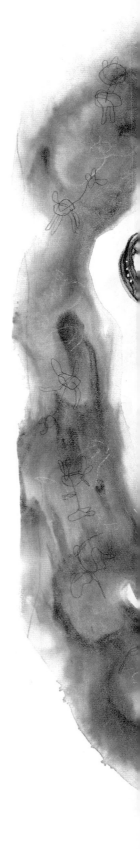

You crawl closer. You reach out a hand. The tips of your fingers tingle at the first touch of feathers. Moving even closer, you curl up beside the bird. There is warmth beneath the feathers. You wait. Breathe in, breathe out.

You drift into sleep. A dream carries you far away to the north, to a wide open place. You see an egg crack. The tip of a tiny, wet beak pokes through. Breathe in, breathe out. Not a murmur, not a movement.
Then the egg wobbles. All at once every part of the tiny body within explodes with a furious energy, pushing in all directions.

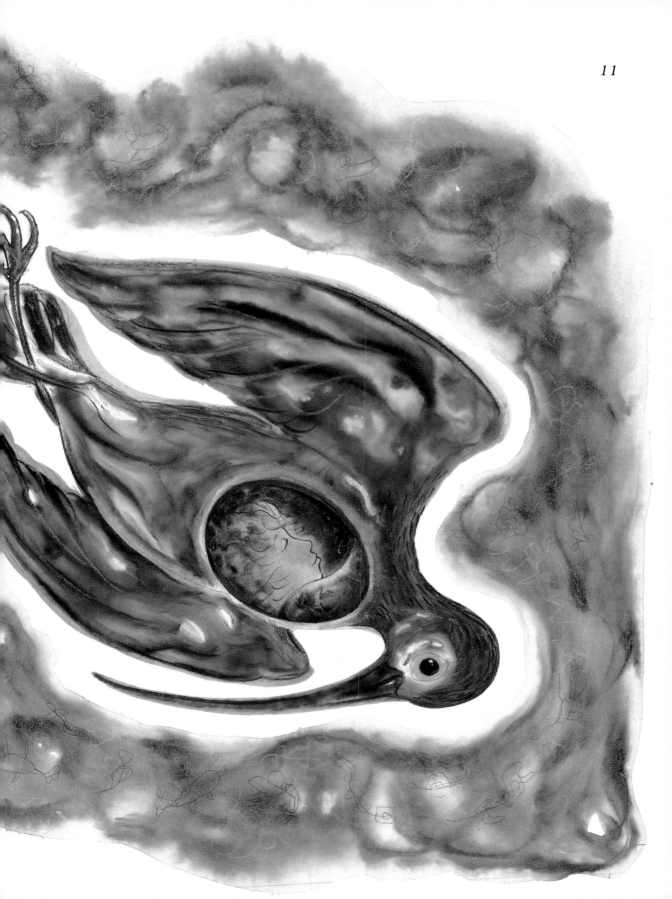

The shell holds tight.
Legs kick harder, head and neck
push and prod, beak pokes, back and
shoulders bump at the shell. Suddenly, with a rush,
the egg splits, spilling a wet bundle onto the dry grass.
A chick is born. A curlew chick.

In your dream, you rest on the earth, cushioned
between nested grasses and warm mother feathers. The
smells are new, different from your big brother's
blankets, and yet familiar. The eyes of the chick are
wide. So wide. Watching. Breathe in, breathe out.
Listening for distant sounds beyond time. Waiting.

The sun yawns and stretches over a vast horizon.
The chick wakes to the sound of a marshland bursting
with life. Shrieks, the flurry of wings, croaks, gurgles,
buzzes, burps, cries on the wind, hungry mouths to feed,
rustling and shaking and shimmering.

Time passes quickly. Dampness dries to down.
Small bird feet scramble to find their place on the
earth. You watch the chick tumble towards the light and
the loudness, pushing away from the safety of mother
and nest. One step and a stumble, two then a flop.
You chew your nails. Three steps, then four, five and six.
You chew harder, knowing your mother is too far away
to tell you to stop. Six and a run. Then the chick
collapses in a bundle of fluff. Your fingers hurt. You
help her back to the nest. With beak stretched wide the
chick drinks the berry juice her mother brings. Together
you drift to sleep.

You follow bird tracks out across the mud. The curlew chick is growing strong and hurries to keep up with her mother. You watch the chick watching each step of the mother bird as she probes the mud with a long, slender beak, elegantly pulling up crabs to eat. Then the chick dips her small beak into the wet earth and quickly out again, shaking away a mouthful of mud and grit. Once more and then again. You are there when the curlew chick pulls up her first catch. Squeezing it tight, she runs round in circles as startled as the young crab dangling from her beak. She stops and takes a gulp. Then swallows. Nothing. The crab is gone. Fallen back to earth and safely down the nearest hole.

You see the feathers grow through her down. Wings form that stretch against the wind. The morning air is sharp as you watch the chick run across the mud, wings flapping. The mother bird runs ahead. You run to keep up with them, leaping and dancing with the wind in your hair. The feet of the curlew chick are still running, her wings flapping fast, when a puff of wind lifts her into the air. Flapping, flapping and calling, the chick tilts, falling, then up again. You wave and shout and urge her on. She dips to the side, on and then flop! Her wings lose control and she lands in a heap on the mud. But the curlew chick has felt the air beneath her wings. You know from your own bumps and scabs her thrill of taking to the sky.

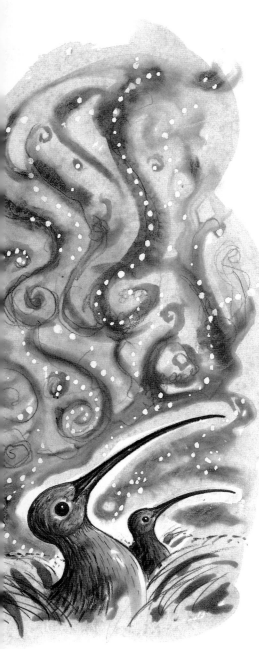

Then a dawn arrives that brings with it something new. You can't see what it is but something in the wind is different. A strangeness rolling in across the treeless marsh, shaking the grasses until they whisper wild things. Coming closer, making the bushes panic and the quiet waters crinkle and shiver with excitement. Leaves and loose things fly into the air. Everything is turning about.

You feel the flock grow restless. Some, then others, call to the wind. Older birds that know arch their necks, spreading their wings to the oncoming rush. Stepping out, dancing, whirling, calling, loosening themselves from the earth.

The mother bird rushes past you, drawn into the flock. Running after her the chick is jostled and bumped. You try to hide but are caught up in a hundred voices that become one deafening cry. The chick runs faster, searching for a familiar shape and smell. She is rushing, confused. Then the flock is startled and all about adult birds are tossed together onto the wind. A million feathers beat the air, birds surge forward and up — eyes, beaks, legs, stretching back, struggling for balance — finally forming a vee that carries the mother bird away across the setting sun.

In your dream you wait with the curlew chick, glued to the mud. Watching. Listening. Missing your mother. Breathe in, breathe out.

Others have been left. Young ones with only the wide arc of sky for shelter. So wide. As the last light drains from the sky you nestle close to the young curlew and drift into an uneasy sleep. You want to be back where the blankets are warm and tucked in. But the dream sticks to you.

The young curlew wakes with a start. The first night has passed with only the moon and stars as a cover. The dawn, still loud with shrieks, croaks, gurgles, buzzes, burps, shaking and shimmering, sounds empty. The tracks across the mud are strangers, the crabs hard to catch.

Days spread out and the nights fold in more easily. Then another dawn brings with it that strange feeling rolling in across the marsh. This time you see the young curlew stepping out — dancing, whirling and calling. Other young birds spin past. You rush to join them. The noise becomes deafening as hundreds of voices call to the wind. Bodies turn faster, then prance and lift. You push through, searching for the young curlew but the earth beneath your feet spins into sky.

Suddenly, a hundred birds are tossed as one onto the wind. You call out. The voice you hear back is loud and raucous, screeching like a cockatoo but shaped into words. Words like the language of your mother and brother. The voice you hear is yours like you have never heard it. Calling out.

'Don't leave me. I want to go with you!'

*T*hen you are a bird. In your dream you fly higher and higher. Looking back, you see the marsh become a patch, then just a speck in a wide stretch of wilderness. Soon it drops over the horizon forever.

Your wings are the wings of the young curlew. Pushing down proudly against the wind, rising up quickly with the rush of air beneath them, pushing down again, quickly up and solidly down, stroking the air. You follow in the current made by those that fly ahead.

You notice that different birds take their turn at the front of the vee. Some are more able than others and take longer turns. Then the bird ahead drops back and there you are, a young curlew taking the lead, alone, facing the wide arc of empty sky. The full strength of the wind thrusts against your body. You strain forward, parting the air, setting the pace, riding the wind. The joy rises in you. You open your long, slender beak just enough to call out in a voice as clear as the Arctic air.

'Mum, look at me. No hands!'

Soaring above the earth, you lead the flock with new effort and grace. An ache settles into one wing then the other. You refuse to give in, you want to stay leader. Your muscles grow weak. Finally you can bear it no longer. You drop back to the tail of the flock and an easier path.

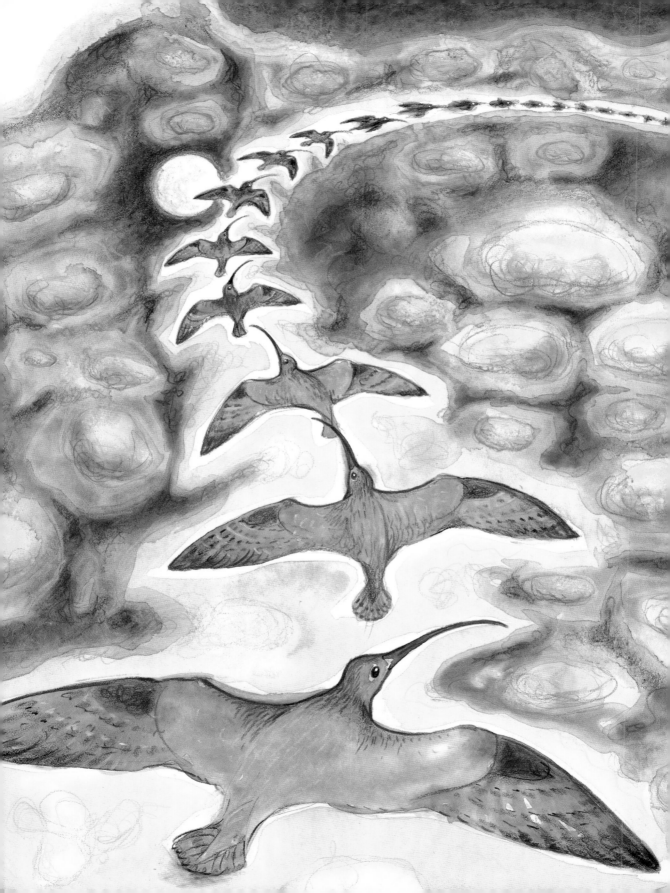

Through days and nights you fly on and on. Then
slowly the flock drifts down to the welcome speck of
mud that stretches out into a wide expanse of shore at
the mouth of a mighty river. You notice flocks of other
birds settled here, resting and feeding.

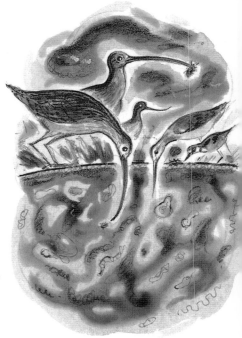

Your curlew feet touch down lightly on the mud.
You plunge a well-curved beak into the wet earth. The
dryness in your throat grates on the first mouthful. You
gulp for more, drinking and digging and filling your
belly with food. In this unfamiliar place you are happy
to wade close to the flock by day, roosting in a huddle
on drier land by night.

The food is good. As good as banana custard or
icy-poles on a hot day. You feel your curlew body grow
strong again and plump. You wander further across the
mud, eyeing other birds for a half-remembered shape, a
slender neck, a curved beak and a warm smell. You see
many other birds, some with beaks like the mother bird
you search for, others with funny beaks that turn up,
and some with short, stubby ones. You wade further,
noticing how tall you stand beside the others, hearing
the calls of different birds and becoming bold.

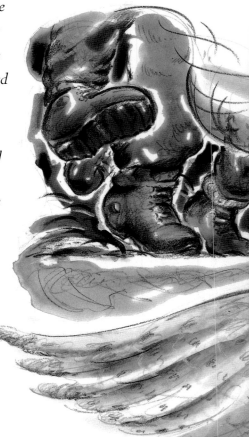

It happens so quickly. You barely hear the whistle
of the hunter's net as it slices through the sky. The
startled shrieks of thousands of birds lift you into the
air in fright. Before your wings can spread you fall
back on the mud, caught by a net that bends back
feathers and bites at flesh. Others are caught too.

Many others crying out and thrashing, becoming more tangled the harder they try to go free.

Heavy feet come running closer, pounding the mud and shouting in thick voices. In your dream these people are like creatures you have never seen before. Their breath is hot and you feel afraid as they grab the net. They tug at the other end. You hear wings flapping then silence, a stifled cry then a dull thud on the earth and a final sigh of breath. The sound makes you shudder and crouch closer to the earth. Listening. Waiting. Breathless. Watching as feathers of the dead lift like spirits on the breeze.

Then the big hands grasp you from behind. They smell of death. Their hold is tight as they bend back your wings, tugging your long, slender beak and wrenching your thin legs out of the net. Their thick voices laugh as they hold you high in the air. You try to call out, to tell them you are really just a child, but you can find no voice. To them you are a curlew, the biggest of the birds that wade in the mud and your flesh is sweet. You are a good catch.

Their laughter is loud. The heavy hands loosen ever so slightly. Quickly you jerk your legs back. One leg breaks free. You claw and scratch the naked skin

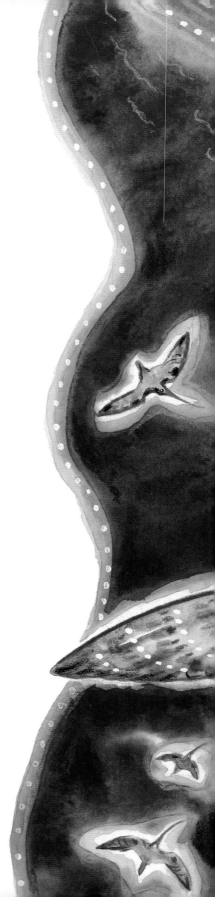

of the hunter. He yells with pain. In a blind rush you hurl yourself clear. Beating wings and thrashing your beak you take to the air like a mad thing, jerking from side to side, up then dropping down, then up again, straining every muscle to climb onto the wind.

Up the beach and across the mouth of the river you fly as if you will never come down. You wish your brother could save you from this nightmare. The sky is dark, everywhere looks strange and full of danger. You keep flying. Finally your damaged wings can go no further. You fall from the sky, landing heavily, then scramble up the beach to hide among the rocks. Here you huddle out of sight, hurt and alone.

The dream shifts. Your wings are stroking the wind again, pushing solidly down then quickly up. You are flying further, following the leader, a part of the flock. An ache in one wing reminds you of danger and makes it hard to keep up. The journey is long. Then with relief you feel a balmy breeze carry you down. You float down from the sky to a quiet stretch of beach. Perhaps you have flown for days across land and sea, struggling through heavy winds under the scorching sun of the equator to the edge of this ancient southern land. You don't know who you are anymore — if you are a bird, or a child, or if this dream will ever end.

A blue, blue sea laps at the deep red earth. As the tide breathes in and out, you join thousands of birds who run behind the waves to feast on creatures left uncovered. As the tide chases you all back up the

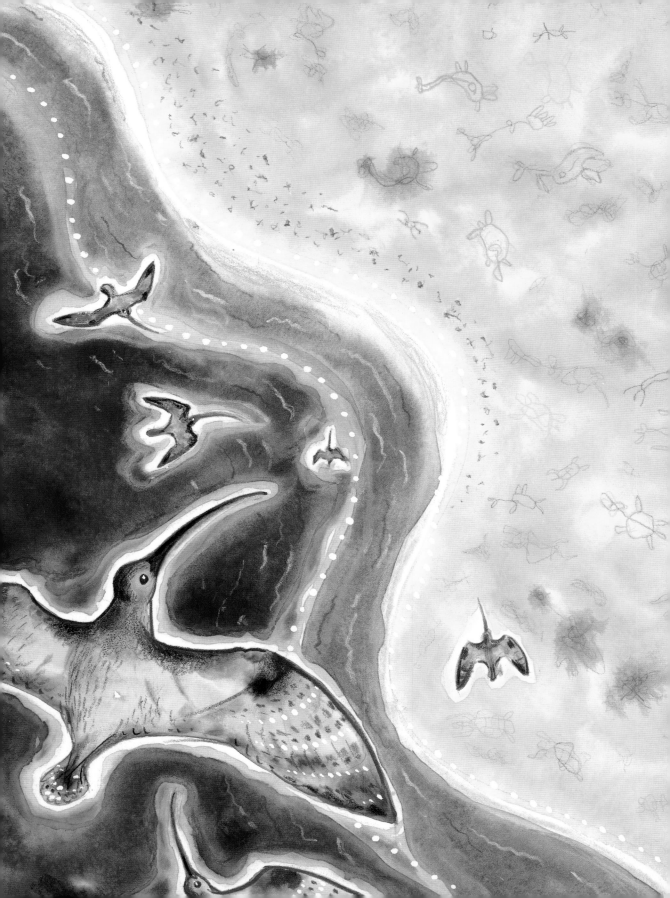

beach you skip ahead, dancing. The froth, like lace,
sinks into sand at your feet. You grow strong again and
plump. The days are peaceful and the nights warm.

As the sun grows heavy and slips over the horizon,
singing rises on the wind. You smell smoke from a
distant fire. You've made friends with a small group of
other birds and enjoy being one of the mob. Together
you wander up the beach and then further, crossing the
dunes. The red, red sand is cooling as the evening fades
to dark. On the next rise you stop still. Completely still.
Breathless. Long shadows dance out from the flickering
fire. The long shadows of those with heavy feet and
thick voices. The others wander closer. You warn them
to stay away.

The sky closes in. You are scared of the dark but
hang back. Nothing will make you go closer to the
dancing shadows. Not even the taunts of the other
birds. You wait, listening for the sound that whistles as
it slices through the sky. Broad, fleshy feet stomp in
time to a sharp clicking rhythm. Clouds of dust curl
into the air. You watch as the long arms of these
creatures spread like wings. They move lightly on legs
stretched by the story they tell. Their bodies bend
forward as if probing the mud with delicately curved
beaks. Their singing and dancing takes to the sky. You
forget your fear and soar with them in spirit. Then you
remember and shrink back into the shadows until silence
settles over the last of the singing and the fire dies away.
The other birds wander back. You hurry them along and
retrace your steps to roost on a distant beach.

*T*he dream carries you on. Again you
are flying, stroking the wind solidly down and
then quickly up, flying endlessly over a huge, brown
land. Then you see the edge of green earth drop down
to a cold, blue sea. The smell of salt and the promise of
wet mud strengthens your wings to push through the
wind. Your eyes strain looking for the spot that will
become a patch and then an expanse of mud. You can
see a distant clutter of shapes, like boxes, painted on
the horizon in hazy blues and greys. The closer
you fly the bigger the boxes become until they
are buildings stretching to the sky.

You follow the leader closer and closer until
there is no telling where one building begins and ends.
Down you fly, tired and hungry, past chimneys that
smoke and through smells that almost take your
breath away. Still you can see only surfaces that
dazzle and hear only the roar of traffic. You want to
roar back at the noise to quieten down and let you
think. The flock banks and turns, sweeping round low.
Suddenly you see a strip of mud tucked in
beneath a towering bridge, beside
a long line of
factories.

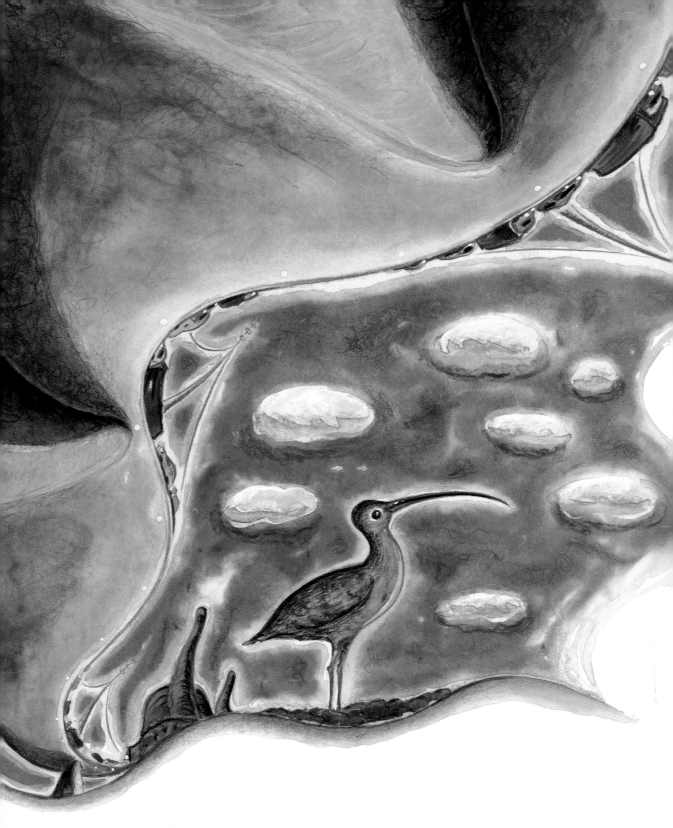

24

Then the wet earth is beneath your feet and your beak plunges into the welcoming mud.

The sounds at dawn are new to you now. So are the colours and shapes during the day. At night you learn to sleep in the afterglow of city lights.

Those with heavy feet and thick voices race past on wheels. A small group of these people wander into your dream. They are busy and seem harmless. Their young ones run and jump, throwing balls and playing games on the grass nearby. A very young one is lying on her blanket in the shade. You know this one. You know how she struggles to roll over, to reach out to her brother with the cheeky, round face and how she sings with the birds. She calls to you. Her voice is raucous, like a cockatoo. You long to fly across, to be out of this dream and back to being that child. But your curlew wings won't move. Your long, thin legs stick in the mud. The child rolls towards you but is gathered up by her mother and carried away. You try to wake up, to call out, but the dream holds you tight.

You feel restless and annoyed with this place. You want to move on. Your curlew wings spread to the oncoming rush and you whirl and dance onto the wind. You watch yourself fly further south, crossing the sea to reach a small stretch of earth which rises out of a wild ocean. Here in a quiet place you finally rest.

Days and weeks, months, maybe a year disappears in your dream. Now you are a full-grown bird. The sun is shrinking from this quiet place in the south and the chill wind makes you want to dance and whirl. Rust-coloured feathers cover your body. You feel a deep yearning to make a nest close to the earth, surrounded by early morning shrieks, the flurry of wings, croaks, gurgles, buzzes, burps, cries on the wind, hungry mouths to feed, rustling and shaking and shimmering. You sense a place far to the north on the edge of memory where you must return.

The dawn comes that tosses you into the air and onto the wind with a flock of birds headed north. You leave the quiet place rising out of the wild sea and fly back over to the patch of mud beneath the towering bridge, beside the chimneys that smoke. You feed and rest here then are off across the huge, brown land flying for days until you float down to the beach and the blue, blue sea. More food and more rest. And then again you fly across sea and land, travelling north until you see the mouth of the mighty river. Reluctantly you come to rest. Cautiously you eat from the mud. Eagerly you wait for the dawn and fly on. You fly further and further north. One morning in the distance you see the curve of a vast horizon stretching over a marshland. A fresh Arctic wind thrusts against your tired body. You strain forward. Longing strengthens your wings to keep pushing down, quickly up and then solidly down. Finally you land back where you began.

The crabs have grown bigger and the berries full of juice. You show off, parading through the many flocks of curlew spread across the marsh. In your dream you laugh at yourself. A curlew with a slender beak and a particular arch to his neck attracts your attention. You giggle, realising that maybe it's his full flush of fine, rust-coloured feathers that you like so much. He calls to you in an irresistible tone. As he moves closer you notice his limp and can tell he knows the hardships of the journey. Turning sideways you casually stretch your wings. He stretches too, then leaps into the air and dives back down. Now you giggle so much that your sides ache and you wake up.

Your eyes open, the sky is blue and the feathers beside you still warm. You are a child again, lying on the ground. You close your eyes quickly, hoping to slip back into the dream. And once more you are a curlew in the marshland with your mate.

Three green, speckled eggs lie cushioned on the grass beneath. You nestle over them, giving warmth. Watching. Listening for distant sounds beyond time. Waiting. Breathe in, breathe out. Finally the first egg cracks and the tip of a tiny, wet beak pokes through.

You are now a mother curlew. You enjoy being followed across the mud by your chicks, and laugh when you think of the look on your big brother's face if he could see you now. The dawn yawns over the horizon, bringing with it that urge to move on.

There is nothing you can do to stay. You who were once left now leave, climbing onto the wind, struggling for a place in the vee. Your young ones cry out as you are carried away with the flock across the setting sun.

You follow the invisible pathway in the sky with ease. Wary of the hunters; feeding behind the waves, resting on the red, red earth; pacing yourself across the huge, brown land, you make the journey south. You are flying towards the buildings like boxes painted on the horizon, knowing that the closer you fly the bigger they become. You know that you are tired and hungry. You know it is time to come to ground to rest and feed on the small strip of mud beneath the towering bridge, beside the chimneys that smoke. You close your ears to the noise and hope the young child will still be there by the bay.

Easing down with the flock, you bank and turn, sweeping round low. But something is wrong. Something has changed. The flock lifts and circles. Again you sweep down to land. The mud is not there. The mud has gone, crusted over by a busy road that roars. The rush and the roar beat you away. You follow the other birds as they lift and turn, searching in wider and wider circles for another place to rest. The confusion of roads and tall buildings leaves no other place. The journey becomes too long. With each turn you see more birds waste and lag behind.

The vee formation becomes loose as each bird longs for a resting place that can't be found.

Then you feel the wind slip through your wings. You try to stroke solidly down and then quickly up but

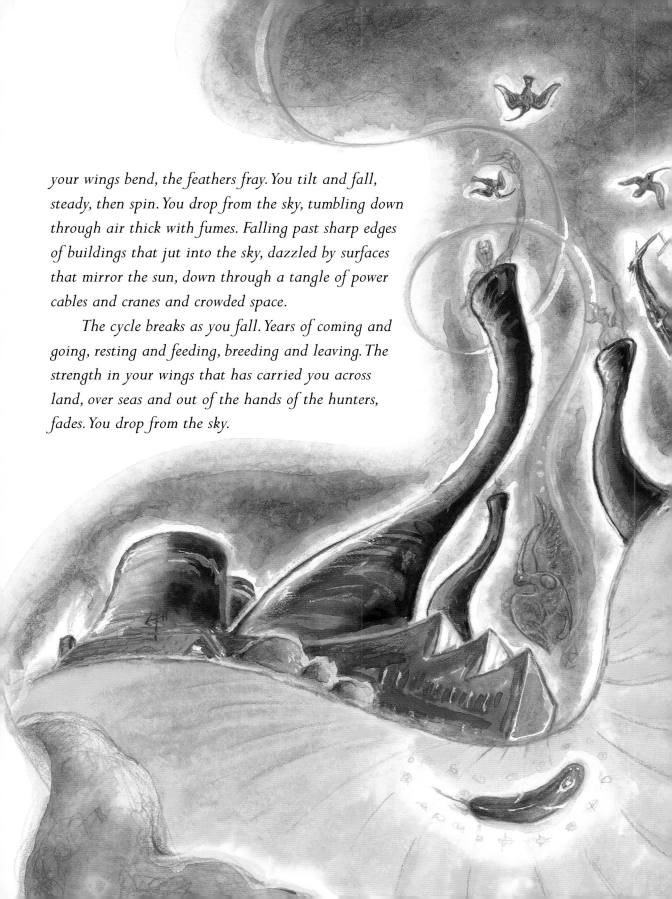

your wings bend, the feathers fray. You tilt and fall, steady, then spin. You drop from the sky, tumbling down through air thick with fumes. Falling past sharp edges of buildings that jut into the sky, dazzled by surfaces that mirror the sun, down through a tangle of power cables and cranes and crowded space.

The cycle breaks as you fall. Years of coming and going, resting and feeding, breeding and leaving. The strength in your wings that has carried you across land, over seas and out of the hands of the hunters, fades. You drop from the sky.

You wake from the dream with a jolt. You move a finger, wriggle your toes and rub your eyes. In that breathless moment between wake and sleep you look up. The sky is still blue but the feathers beside you have lost their warmth. You want to hold the curlew closer, to shut your eyes and fly with her again. A chill in the air makes you shiver. You must find your feet and move about. The dead bird, the curlew fallen from the sky, stays lying on the ground.

The sun is sinking. You clear a space beside the curlew. Beneath the rubble the earth is dark and warm, moist and full of secrets. You grab an old plank of wood and push into the soil. The earth gives way. You dig a hole deep and wide enough to hold the big curlew. You gather blades of grass for a lining. Hoping your mother isn't watching, you pick bright-faced daisies, sunny balls of wattle, even a gardenia that draws you close with its velvet scent. You dig the grave wider so that you can make a bed of flowers like wings for the bird.

You choose a twig, just the right twig, to draw patterns like bird tracks on the fresh earth. Pebbles scatter. You finger the knot of the necklace your brother made from feathers and things. The string of treasures falls free. There are the bright feathers of parrots, the speckled browns of pigeons, the jet black of crows and, right in the middle, the biggest is white with a sulphur yellow tip. Between each

feather are deep red and clear, clear blue beads that catch the light. You fiddle with your favourite feathers and roll the beads between your fingers, thinking back to the dream.

You push back the rubble to make more room. Setting each feather at its best angle you place the necklace on the ground in a circle above the flower wings. You gather up the curlew in your arms. As you lay her to rest you feel a sound stirring inside. You open your mouth to let it out.

> *Kaar kaaaaar kaka*
> *Ka ka kaaaaar kaaw*

You spread your arms wide to the sky. Your legs stretch long and thin as you dance. Your cockatoo song rises on the wind.

> *Kaaaka karoh karraar*
> *Kaawaar kaakoo karaw*

Your brother rushes in from school with a friend. They scramble around in the kitchen feeding, then push and shove their way outside. They stop when they hear you up the back. They watch for a moment as you sing and dance. Your brother is embarrassed and turns to go inside. From the corner of your eye you see them and race across the yard to drag him back.

He is angry now but you don't care. You make them follow you to where the curlew lies. As soon as they see the magnificent bird they stop pulling away and crouch down to take a closer look. You clap a rhythm, tapping your feet in time.

Kaaaar ka kar ka ka
Kaaaaaaaaar kaaaaro

The friend begins to snigger. You spin round. Your look makes him swallow his laughter. He almost chokes on his chewing gum. Coughing and spluttering, his hands begin to clap in rhythm. Your brother finds his own feet dancing in time.

Ka ka kaar kaar kaaro
Kaaaaaa kaar kaaaaro

The rhythm picks up. In a corner of the garden where the fence is falling down the neighbour's children peek through. Giggling a bit, they clamber over and join in. Your mother comes out of the house. She watches for a while, then her feet start tapping. Dust lifts and curls into the air.

The fence creaks as the neighbour leans over to see what the children are doing. You mime digging in the ground while your brother calls out.

'You got a shovel? Can you come and help us dig?'

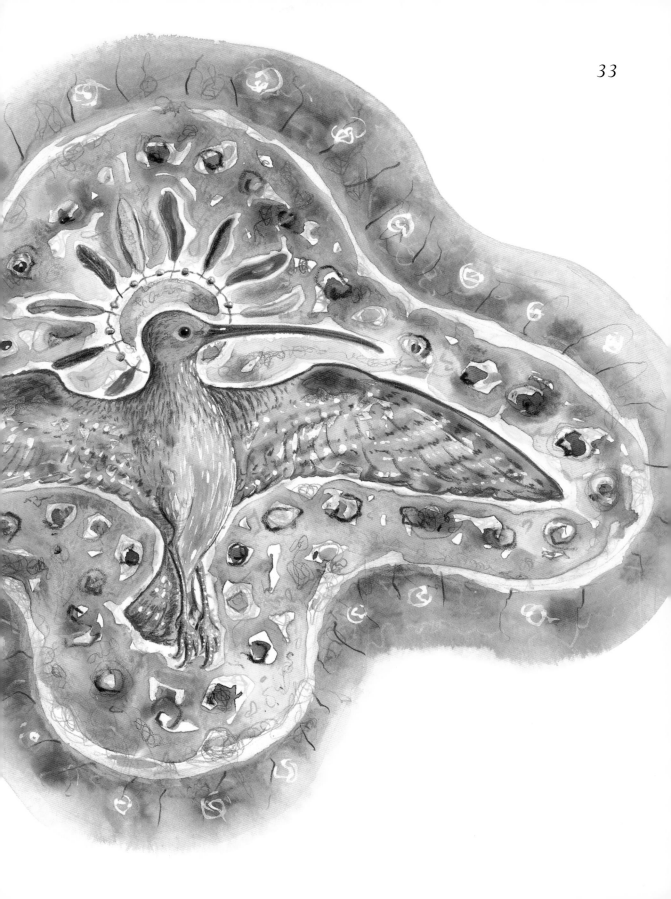

She laughs, then shrugs, why not? With eyebrows raised, your mother opens the door for the neighbour You start them clearing the rubble into piles and digging the grave wider and deeper. They are half-hearted at first. You push them to work faster.

Together you keep working until dark clouds roll across the sun, thunder rumbles, the wind blows and lightning splits the sky into rain. The first drops are heavy and hot on your cheeks. Scooping up a handful of earth, you gather the others around the dead bird. The dark earth falls from your hands. More hands scoop the earth up and let it fall, covering the curlew. As if the sky can hold its tears no longer, the rain pours down.

The neighbour and her children scatter over the fence. Your mother runs inside. You grab your brother and go straight to his bike. He can see there is no use arguing. Through the rain he pedals with you as fast as he can round the block to old man cockatoo. When you get there, the door is flapping on its hinges. The cage is empty.

Long into the night the wild storm rages. You climb onto the top bunk and curl up with your brother. Calm returns with the morning. You wake up early. It's the weekend so you leave him sleeping while you tiptoe out the back.

Where the bird lies buried a pool of water has formed. You slide your feet out of their slippers and creep the toes, big ones first, into the wet.

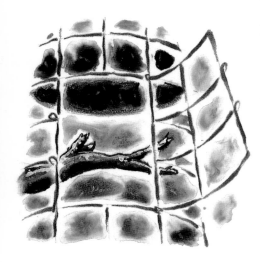

Mud oozes between piggy-went-to-market and this-one-stayed-at-home. The sound pushes up again, shaping your mouth in new ways.

Maar ka maar ka maar...

In the storm a corner of the old fence fell down. The children from next door clear away the palings and sneak through. Together you begin to work again. Your brother comes out and soon his best friend is over. He shares his chewy round. All day you mound the rubble, covering it with dirt, making bigger banks to hold the water.

As more rain falls, the pool grows deeper and wider. Your mother invites other neighbours over. Friends drop in. The old fence keeps falling down. And you keep practising.

Maar ka maar ka maar
Maar ka maar ka...may...

Spring grows into summer. Someone's father builds a seat from the fence palings. Now lots of pathways weave from one home to another. Summer cools down to autumn. A gardener who lives two doors down knows about plants that like wet places. A day is chosen for planting and everyone comes to help, then stays on. Your mother laughs and makes a special cake. Even the cranky old bloke from up the back comes and mumbles in the corner.

The sun slides away and it's time to go inside. You slip past the others to take one more look at the pool. You hear a familiar screech and look up. Old man cockatoo sits picking his toenails in a nearby tree. You sing out to him.

Maar ka maar ka may
May...may...may...

Winter takes forever. Then you wake one morning to a dawn that feels fresh on the horizon. There is something new that drags you out from between warm sheets to creep down to the mud puddle that has become the local swamp. Frogs croak and tall grasses wave good morning.

At first the browns and buffs are hard to see. Then the shape becomes clearer. A delicate curved beak, a slender neck and long legs. A young curlew sits panting on the edge. Breathe in, breathe out. You watch each other. Eyes wide. So wide.

The young curlew probes a tired beak into the mud and draws up a crab. Joy rises in you. With it comes a new voice as fresh and clear as the Arctic wind.

You open your mouth wide and sing to the sky.

Kaar ka kaar ka maar
    Maar ka maar ka may
        May kircle may circle meet
            May bring you here to stay

May the rush be in the wind
    May the berries grow on trees
        May the tracks we make together
            Feed our longing to be free

May the sun stay in the sky
    May the fish be in the sea
        May the earth be ever round
            That circles you and me

May the waves stay in the ocean
    May the sky be overhead
        May the wings be there to carry
            Us safely to our bed

Now the words within me speak
    May I still know how to say
        Kaar ka kaar ka maar
            Maar ka maar ka may

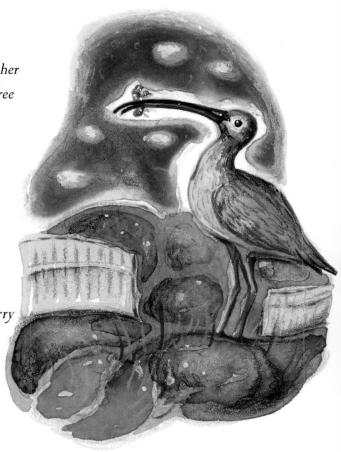

Much later you walk back into the house. Your mother is busy making breakfast.

'Mum…'

It is the first word she has ever heard you speak. The cup of tea in her hand drops to the floor and splatters everywhere. She doesn't seem to mind. She laughs and cries and hugs you until you can hardly breathe.

Each morning you join the curlew at dawn. While you dip into a bowl of cereal, the curlew probes the mud. Sometimes your brother wanders out rubbing the sleep from his eyes. He has made friends with the frogs and likes to stroke their slippery backs or look for tadpoles growing legs. You see neighbours walk out into the fresh morning for a stretch before they get ready for their busy days. The cranky old bloke from up the back mumbles to old man cockatoo perched in the gum tree and he screeches back.

Your days are busy too. Along with all the other children you hurry to school in the mornings. You pack your coloured pencils into their case, twirling them between your fingers and watching the colours spin. Words become your language. You roll your tongue round new sounds. Sometimes it's a struggle to make the thoughts fit the words and you get angry and tired. At the end of the day you return to the quiet spot by the swamp to sing. Listening. Watching. Your mind soars on the wings of a bird that flies overhead.

One morning as you wander out for breakfast you feel something different in the air. Something strange comes rolling in from the north. You watch the curlew more closely. When your mother calls out to get ready for school, you wait just a few moments longer, to sing a farewell to the curlew.

May the winds carry you safely
May the stars be your guide
May the wetlands be there waiting
When you reach the other side

May our hearts travel with you
May our spirits learn to fly
May our feet touch down lightly
On the earth, sea and sky

May our voices join the singing
May our feet dance through the day
Kaar ka kaar ka maar
Maar ka maar ka may

The next morning you wake before the dawn.
You make breakfast knowing there is no rush.
You walk beside the swamp to the empty
patch where the curlew used to wade in
the mud.

Reflections dance across the water. You imagine the curlew flying high above the city joining a flock headed north. Your mind's eye flies ahead, across the great expanse of brown land you know well as Australia, to the beach in Broome. Then high above the islands of Indonesia, along Malaysia and across the South China Sea, to follow the coast around Vietnam to China. You see the curlew settling on the soft mud at the mouth of the mighty Yangtse River. Still further you go, to the treeless marshland of Siberia bursting with life, where the mosquitoes are starting to buzz and the spring flowers are opening in pinks and yellows.

The eye of your mind seeks out wetlands stretched round the world like pearls in a sparsely strung necklace. Beside each wetland you see people sleeping, stretched out in the cool of the evening, others curled up against the cold. You reach out to shake them awake, to tell them the birds are coming, to ask them to look out for the curlew and keep her safe.

The people of your dream fade but the vision stays with you, making you leap up and run inside to your brother.

'Come on, wake up! We've got to send messages to them! Get out of bed!'

Yawning and complaining your brother slides down from the top bunk.

'What are you talking about? Why don't you go back to talking cockatoo! You made more sense then.'

You lead off up the street to school with your brother and friends from next door following. You reach the principal's office well before the bell. When the door opens, there you are at the front of the group. You remember leading the curlew flock in your dream. Now it is up to you to do the talking.

Your voice is clear, as clear as the Arctic air. You tell him the story of the birds, how far they fly, and the resting places they need to make their migration. You have to let people know. Before the first bell rings the principal is convinced. A special time in the day is set aside so that the whole school can make postcards. This time as the birds fly north, messages are sent ahead from one place to the next.

The curlew just left our place.
Have you seen them arrive?
Is there space for the birds near you?

Beneath the towering bridge beside the bay, voices of
the Yarra Yarra and Wurundjeri people can
be heard telling their children.

Koyuparter karbonen kundee narroon?
Take care of the birds, look after them.
Warregerri koyuparter karboneit.

*Wandeet nganggak warrkoneit brimbonga
kruk-wor-rum perit-perit duwi mundagat
miamba.* Come listen. Look. Find the long-
nosed water bird. Go protect them from harm.

By the beach in Broome, children, friends,
neighbours, grandparents, aunties and uncles come
out of their homes to welcome the birds. The Yawuru
people listen for the curlew and tell their stories.

Nyamba bandalmada nilawarl guwaa.
This bird name curlew.
Nyamba bandalmada juwarri wayingarr-ngara.
This bird, if they are going to die
then we are all dead. *Gala yadirri juwarri.*

Nyamba mabu bandalmada. These good birds.
Malu mabu juwarri wayingarr-ngara.
Not good if they are going to die.
Take care of the birds. All you people
look after this place for the birds, for us all.

Beside the mighty Yangtse River people wait to see if the birds will come.

晚的 喃嘴 哇狂阿 覓播嘴 哭我裸 扎熱-扎熱 度爲 慢達嘴 秘阿白
來 聽 看 找到 長鼻子水鳥 去 保護 他們 不要 傷害 他們

Listen, quiet, be still. The birds will come.

Wait. Our place is their place.

Leave space for the birds.

Far to the north beside the marshlands the call can be heard.

Мы позаботимся о твоих яйцах.

Строй своё гнездо в травах.

Мы обеспечим сохранность твоих птенцов.

We will take care of your eggs.

Build your nests amongst the grasses.

We will make sure your chicks are safe.

An egg cracks and the tip of a tiny, wet beak pokes through. Eyes wide. Watching. Breathe in, breathe out. Waiting. Listening for the sounds beyond time.

The echo is heard across the world. Way to the south the Maori elders welcome the birds.

E nga mau, kua whakatakotohia
te ara o nga tupuna, nau mai hoki mai!
To the birds that lay forth our ancestral pathways,
we welcome your return.

We welcome the birds, they are our family.
He powhiritia ki nga manu ko ratou ra
to tatou whanau. He kotahi wairua!
We are one spirit!

The voices join together. Breathe in and breathe out.
Watch for the birds…listen for the birds…for the
birds…*maar ka may*…

The Eastern Curlew

Every year, all over the world, many birds migrate from their feeding grounds to other places for breeding. Some of these birds move only small distances from coastal areas to inland swamps, for example. Others travel vast distances between continents across the globe.

The migratory wading birds sustain a life of endless summer. They breed in the northern hemisphere in the middle of the year and return south for the rest of the time, often to the same wetland they have visited year after year.

The Eastern Curlew breeds in Siberia then flies along the East Asian Australasian Flyway to inter-tidal wetlands around Australia and occasionally as far south as Aotearoa/New Zealand. There are at least another 35 species of birds which regularly migrate along this same Flyway, many travelling from beyond the Arctic Circle. The Eastern Curlew is the largest of the migratory wading birds. As it passes through densely populated regions of Asia it is hunted as a source of food.

To make this journey of approximately 10 000 kilometres, the Eastern Curlew depends on a chain of wetlands on which to rest and feed to regain strength before attempting each further leg. Because of their various feeding methods and the different foods they take, many different species of migratory wading birds can share the same mudflat without significantly competing with each other for food. Like all waders, the Eastern Curlew will increase its body weight by between 40 per cent and 70 per cent before migrating and will lose all of this added weight within two or three days of continuous flying. It may travel up to 5000 kilometres in one flight, reaching a speed of 70 kilometres per hour.

The Eastern Curlew chicks attempt their first migration when they are only six or eight weeks old. Also, they attempt this enormous journey after the adult birds have already departed. These chicks inherit from their parents an innate sense of the direction and distance for their migration.

How the birds navigate on their long migration remains a mystery. One theory suggests that the birds maintain their flight path by alignment with the sun, the moon and the stars. Another theory suggests that they have a particular sensory ability which attunes them to the earth's magnetic field and they set their course accordingly.

Recent comprehensive surveys throughout Australia and along the Flyway have established that the world population of the Eastern Curlew is about 20 000. Some Eastern Curlew have been known to live for more than 20 years, however because of the hazards of migration and the difficulties of finding food the average life expectancy for the young birds is only three or four years.

Waderbirds – Odyssey of the Wetlands

The Way of the Birds was inspired by 'Waderbirds – Odyssey of the Wetlands', the journey of a team of artists who followed the northern migration of the Eastern Curlew. Meme McDonald was the Artistic Director of this team who staged outdoor performances with hundreds of local people to tell the story of the Eastern Curlew through large visual images, music, dance and fire effects. 'Waderbirds' began in Auckland, Aotearoa/New Zealand beside the Manukau Harbour, then crossed the Tasman to Melbourne and on to Broome in Western Australia, finishing in Kushiro on Japan's north island of Hokkaido. This final performance was staged as part of the 1993 meeting of RAMSAR, the International Wetlands Convention to which 87 nations are a signatory.

An education package, *Waderbirds – Odyssey of the Wetlands,* was produced by the Department of Agriculture, Energy and Minerals, East Melbourne, using research conducted on the East Asian Australasian Flyway.

Acknowledgments

Many people have contributed to this book in the years that it has been in the making. My deepest thanks to Shane Nagle for taking the story to heart and for the care with which he has enlivened the words with his inspired illustrations. I would like to especially thank Rosalind Price and Sue Flockhart; all those who worked along the Flyway on 'Waderbirds', in particular Kate Clere, Nell White, Beth Shelton, Tim Newth, Greg Sneddon, and Dr Clive Minton for his generous advice on the birds; and family and friends, Winsome Roberts, Linda Waters, Jill Swanson, Neil Cameron, Rachel Burns, Joy Murphy, Sharyn Prentice, Libby and Caroline Gregory, Chris, Joseph and Grace Lovell, Monty Pryor and Jenny Darling.

Translations

Those who translated text into their own language also contributed much more in terms of an understanding of their land and culture.

Wurundjeri text by Jesse and Ian Hunter and Robert Mate Mate.

Yawuru text by Doris 'Ngaljan' Edgar. Burungu skin group, Yawuru people. Birthplace – Gularbariny aka Injidana Outcamp. Father Yawuru, Mother Garajerri. Yawuru translations by Pat 'Mamajun' Torres. Banaga skin group, Yawuru people. Birthplace – Rubibi aka Broome. Mother – Yawuru.

Maori text by Stephen Bradshaw. Co-director of 'Waderbirds' in Aotearoa/ New Zealand.

Russian text by Pavel Tomkavitch. Consultant on behavior and breeding habits of the Eastern Curlew in Siberia.

Chinese text by Lincoln Wu.

The Way of the Birds

Lyrics by Meme McDonald   Music by Greg Sneddon

Meme McDonald has worked as a theatre and festival director for many years, as well as a photographer and writer. Her first book, *Put Your Whole Self In*, won the 1993 New South Wales State Literary Award for non-fiction, and the audio award in the Braille and Talking Book Library Awards 1993.

Shane Nagle trained as a graphic designer and now works as a freelance illustrator. He has illustrated *We the Earth*, by Katherine Scholes, and a novel for children, *Pumped Up!*, by Mike Dumbleton.

© Text, Meme McDonald 1996
© Illustrations, Shane Nagle 1996

First published 1996
A Little Ark Book
Allen & Unwin Pty Ltd
9 Atchison Street
St. Leonards, NSW 2065
Australia

10 9 8 7 6 5 4 3 2 1

National Library of Australia
Cataloguing-in-Publication entry:

McDonald, Meme, 1954- .
  The way of the birds: a child and a curlew travel across the world
  ISBN 1 86448 027 0 (hb)
  ISBN 1 86448 026 2 (pb)
  1. Curlews - Juvenile fiction.
  I. Nagle, Shane. II. Title.
  A823.3

Designed by Sandra Nobes
Typeset in Perpetua by Tou-Can Design
Printed in Hong Kong by Wing King Tong Co. Ltd

'The Way of the Birds' – Lyrics © Meme McDonald
Music composed by Greg Sneddon, © Copyright Warner/Chappell Music Australia Pty Ltd